T0057364

LIFE LESSONS FROM A HOMEMADE SOURDOUGH STARTER

LIFE LESSONS
from a
HOMEMADE SOURDOUGH STARTER

TEACHINGS IN HAPPINESS WITH
THE ONE & ONLY SOURDOUGH RECIPE

Judith Stoletzky *&* Lutz Geißler

TILLER PRESS

NEW YORK   LONDON   TORONTO   SYDNEY   NEW DELHI

TILLER PRESS

An Imprint of Simon & Schuster, Inc.
1230 Avenue of the Americas
New York, NY 10020

Copyright © 2018 by Becker Joest Volk Verlag GmbH & Co. KG

Text and visual concept by Judith Stoletzky
Idea and recipes by Lutz Geißler
Photography by Hubertus Schüler
Translated by Judith Stoletzky
Graphic design by Judith Stoletzky & Inga Detlow

Originally published in Germany in 2018 by Becker Joest Volk Verlag GmbH & Co. KG as
Ca. 750 g Glück: Das kleine Buch von der großen Lust sein, eigenes Sauerteigbrot zu backen

First Tiller Press hardcover edition February 2021

TILLER PRESS and colophon are trademarks of Simon & Schuster, Inc.

For information about special discounts for bulk purchases, please contact
Simon & Schuster Special Sales at 1-866-506-1949 or business@simonandschuster.com.

The Simon & Schuster Speakers Bureau can bring authors to your live event.
For more information or to book an event, contact the Simon & Schuster Speakers Bureau
at 1-866-248-3049 or visit our website at www.simonspeakers.com.

Manufactured in the United States of America

1   3   5   7   9   10   8   6   4   2

Library of Congress Cataloging-in-Publication Data
Names: Stoletzky, Judith, author.
Title: Life lessons from a homemade sourdough starter / by Judith Stoletzky.
Description: New York : Tiller Press, 2020.
Identifiers: LCCN 2020034580 (print) | LCCN 2020034581 (ebook) |
ISBN 9781982169824 (hardcover) | ISBN 9781982169862 (ebook)
Subjects: LCSH: Cooking (Sourdough) | Sourdough bread. | Fermentation. | LCGFT: Cookbooks.
Classification: LCC TX770.S66 S76 2020 (print) | LCC TX770.S66 (ebook) | DDC 641.81/5—dc23
LC record available at https://lccn.loc.gov/2020034580
LC ebook record available at https://lccn.loc.gov/2020034581

ISBN 978-1-9821-6982-4
ISBN 978-1-9821-6986-2 (ebook)

"If you want to be happy, bake a loaf of bread."

— Lutz Geißler

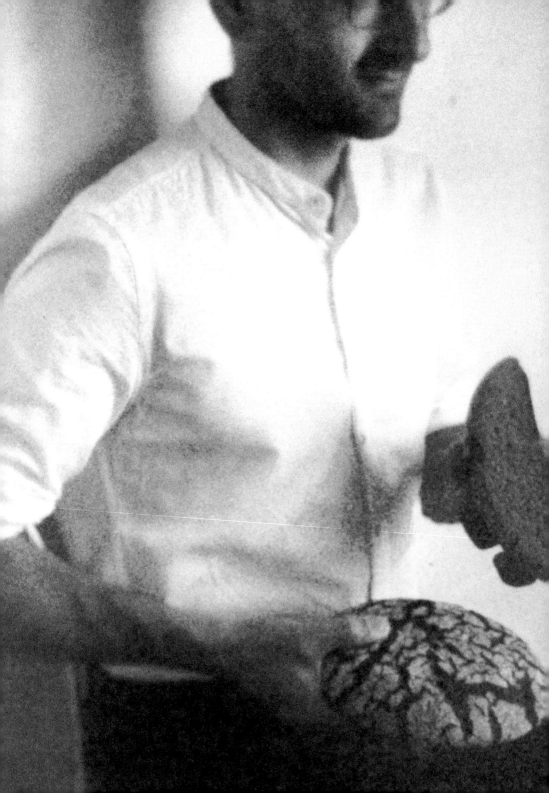

CONTENTS

Foreword

A good teacher
makes you grow.

Do you remember your favorite teacher? Do you remember what this teacher did differently? You probably can't recall his or her actually teaching you lessons. What you learned you likely absorbed through your pores because the teacher sparked a flame that ignited your interest and catapulted you right into the subject by awakening your senses, making you feel, and giving you the bliss of grasping the topic through experience rather than rote drills.

Interested in Happiness, Anyone?

The word interest comes from the Latin *inter* and *esse*. *Inter*, for in the center of or in between, and *esse*, for the verb *to be*. *Interest* means someone is *in* it, in the middle of the matter. *Interest* means becoming one with what you do. Being a part of it. And that's a hell of a happy feeling! This tiny book describes how a vague interest in baking bread turned into an exciting journey into mindfulness and the creation of an easy, everyday recipe for happiness—not through osmosis but through sticky sourdough.

It's Not Always about Dough

Happiness is a term as soft and amorphous as sourdough. It raises questions. Different people have very different concepts of happiness, and our fantasies often come in the shape of kitschy clichés involving mansions, unicorns, eternal youth, yachts, designer handbags, and a fancy car (or twenty fancy cars!). Happiness is often interpreted as more, more, more. But true happiness can be a relaxation into less, less, less. It can even be less than less. The mere absence of things may be abundance.

Feel Rich

The guru this book is inviting you to follow is not really a teacher. He doesn't have a degree, he doesn't speak Latin, he doesn't know a single thing. He's a heavy, lazy, greedy, and sometimes grumpy lump with a slightly sour smell (we all had a teacher like that in high school!). His gray eminence made it very clear from lesson one that we already have all we need to create happiness.

Bread & Circuses

One Bakes.
One Writes.

This book is a serious matter. I created it in response to an impulse from a serious German geoscientist named Lutz Geißler, whose life was turned upside down after he started baking bread. Now he is no longer a geologist but a professional baker. He teaches baking and writes bestselling cookbook after bestselling cookbook. He counsels industrial bakeries and artisan bakers; he teaches gourmet chefs around the globe. Being a scientist, he strives for perfection, and hobbyist bakers can count on his recipes being repeatedly reviewed and verified in serious experimental setups and precisely replicable at home—successfully, deliciously, and beautifully. We learn up to the third decimal place how many grams of which natural ingredient are to be put into what, exactly when, and why. We learn precisely what a dough has to look like, smell like, and feel like.

Even though Lutz is a man of unequivocal facts, while baking, he began to believe in forces whose existence is not easy to prove scientifically. Dough does not always stick to the numbers Lutz first wrote down, and this made him believe in the powers of pure chance. He even believes that dough has a soul and its own will, and that its personality must be respected if we want to transform it into beautiful bread. These are the objective reasons for learning to trust our subjective perception and our senses, as it seems that these instruments offer greater precision. Or is it higher art?

Lutz Was for This Little Book
What a Sourdough Starter Is for Bread

Once baking had, to his own amazement, turned his life and his views around completely, Lutz woke up one day to the insight that the world needed to know, too! We should know how wonderful it is to bake bread, and how little is needed to transform one's self and create a more contented, mindful life. He dreamed of a baking book, but not the type we're used to—small in size but big in meaning, and about something so inexact as happiness. He even mentioned a four-letter word starting with L. There was just one problem: he had no idea what the recipe for a book about feelings instead of facts should be. What were the ingredients, the measurements, the chapters, the images, the words? What to write about, precisely? Which form and shape and taste should it have? So he asked me to create a recipe for a sourdough bread book that would contain just one single recipe. A book that would get people hooked and happy. And he also asked me to bake the thing!

There was only one way to go: I had to experience it all myself. So I took to the unscientific experiment, switching on all my senses and discovering all kinds of amazing feelings. Hopefully you will find the description so tasty that you'll want to try it out yourself. Creating your own sourdough starter. Cuddling it and caring for it. Feeding it. Naming it. Watching it breathe and grow. Trying to understand what it wants to tell you, what it can teach you. When your starter bursts out of the jar with zest for life, burst with joy yourself. And when you pull your very first loaf from the oven, burst with happiness—let the feeling be contagious!

Courage

On the Angst of New Beginnings,
on Simplicity and a Great Poet

The gateway to the irreversible obsession with baking bread opens in a similar way for most of the afflicted. Their first loaf is not baked with the intention of sustaining themselves or their families, nor do they aspire to celebrity status and hope to be proclaimed pope or popess of sourdough. Most of us bake our first loaf with mild curiosity about the outcome, and we bake to unwind. We mix flour and water without adding too much ambition. Edibility of the result is welcome but not a must—and palatability is considered a bold dream. When it comes to bread, we're not used to anything spectacular anyway, and baking something better than what the vast majority of industrial bakeries put out seems easy. Making a decision to bake that first loaf is giving ourselves permission to play—and what's even more relaxing, we don't even feel the need to win! Failure is permitted. It almost reminds us of those long-ago days when we were small and possibly cute, too, baking mud pies in the sandbox, with nothing we need to achieve, forgetting the time and the world around us.

Excitingly Relaxing

As opposed to many other vocations we humans pursue to relax and unwind, baking bread is useful, creative, and nourishing. You can't seriously say this about coloring in adult coloring books; watching TV; liking online posts and posting links; drinking wine; or bossing around kids, partners, and pets. If you free yourself from any pressure to perform by baking the perfect loaf, this activity will be relaxing before you even start. The investment required to embark upon this adventure is very modest. If the plan to become an amateur baker doesn't rise to your expectations, there's little chance of bankruptcy, and you can let go of it without consequence. There's no need to sell a model train set, a double bass, a paraglider, or a drone on Craigslist. It's rather improbable that you will run into the souvenirs of your failures behind the guest room door or in the basement, glaring at you reproachfully.

Some Flour, a Bit of Water, an Ocean of Time

If you are a halfway domesticated being, you might, at this very moment, already have all the equipment you need to get started: water, flour, salt, and a standard oven. If you need golf clubs, koi fish, nude models, or a brush for pollinating orchids, it's a little more cumbersome to transform an energetic impulse into action. Baking bread is clearly more easily accomplished than staging medieval jousting tournaments or performing music in a string quartet.

If you're in desperate need of immediate, instant relaxation, baking bread is possible without any training, teammates, or opponents. You can start spontaneously, in the light of day, or in the midnight hours during one of those sleepless nights, for example, that we all know, when a burning sensation behind our sternum impedes our passage into restful sleep. This burning sensation resembles the feeling we all suffer after noshing too many mono- and diglycerides, when we're too weak to hold back on all those delicious exogenous enzymes—on (*mmmmmm*) pentosanase, proteinase, cellulase and hemicellulase, yummy xylanase, lipoxygenase, glucose oxidase, phospholipase, and maltogenic alpha-amylase. Emulsifiers, stabilizers, humectants—dough improvers of all kinds. Yes, industrial bread is seductive!

So often poor little gluten is shamed for things it very probably did not do. And even artisan whole-grain bread, baked by an honest and well-meaning organic professional, might not necessarily promote sleep if the baker hasn't allowed enough time for the peacemaking lactic-acid bacteria to act upon the harsh substances in the outer layer of the grain. But that burning sensation behind the sternum could also be something that's not entirely physical. It could be a longing. It whispers, "You're missing something." Our souls yearn for something to set us on fire.

Only the Anxious Can Be Courageous

Often on nights like this, after kneading gloomy thoughts for hours and hours, we finally leap into action. We start baking. Overnight it dawns on us to pay more attention to the quality of the ingredients we use in the recipe for our lives. We realize that there may be too much in it that doesn't agree with us, and that less might be more. Often this discovery comes along with the exhilarating insight that finitude is dangling from the ceiling above us and can flop onto the duvet at any time. And then there it is, all of a sudden, the answer to the question "When is the ideal moment to make a change?"

Now!

What human with even a morsel of humanist education doesn't instantly recall this evocative poem by Rainer Maria Rilke? Perhaps you? Let's support your memory and recite it:

Archaic Torso of Apollo

We never saw his phenomenal head
with eyes like ripening apples. Yet,
his torso is still glowing like a chandelier,
retaining his gaze, turned low now,

persistently gleaming. Otherwise the prow of the chest
could not dazzle you so, and the gentle movement
of the loins could not flow like a smile
towards this center that once carried procreation.

Otherwise this stone would stand disfigured
under the sheer dome of the shoulders
and would not glisten like the fur of a beast

and would not, from all its edges,
erupt like a star: there is no spot
that does not behold you. You have to change your life.

And if it's not Rilke you think of, it's Lutz Geißler. You think of this master baker's recipe (conveniently found on page 64), of words that need no interpretation: you think of a recipe for sourdough.

Unlike the sculpture of Apollo, the god of poets and healing (who has only a torso), we have a head and arms and legs and are not made of marble but of flesh and blood. We have the power to take our lives into our own hands. We start with an amorphous mass of flour and water and transform it into delicious bread that nourishes body and soul.

So, we rise from our rumpled bed, right ourselves, slip into our robe, and stride into the kitchen. With the elation of the bleary-eyed, we fish an old screw-top jar out of the recycling bin under the sink. We check the bag of flour for its best-by date, and off we go!

But suddenly there are doubts—not because of the best-by date but because of everything. Because of dear God and the hunger in the world, and the revolutions and the wars that break out because the price of bread is rising in regions where one does not have a choice between 1,323 varieties. Because *it is a big thing* to mix water and flour. We instinctively sense that bread is not the simple sum of its parts. It's more than a mode of transportation for slices of ham and cheese or for peanut butter and jelly. Bread contains more than three ingredients. No food carries more symbolism and more historical culture. He who has no bread has nothing. He who has just bread and water survives.

Relax Yourself, Relax the Dough

With our trembling hands and our agitated mind, we coura-geously mix water and flour into a plaster-like mass. This is our chance to foster trust—in the way of the world, in the unfold-ing of the universe, in other beings, even if they're so small as to be invisible. Water, flour, and confidence can expand into something far greater than sourdough. If, during that fateful night, lactic-acid bacteria, water, and flour, feeling that no one's watching, get closer in that mustard jar, their rendezvous will produce consequences. They reproduce; they want to make many, many beautiful bread babies, and, like all children, none will be like the others.

And something is growing not only in the screw-top jar, under plastic wrap, and in the proofing basket but also in the soul of the fledgling amateur baker. Almost imperceptibly, we arrange our lives around baking, and Lutz Geißler turns out not to be the only one whose life has been turned around completely by baking bread. But don't worry—it's not obligatory to be sleep-less or unhappy to start. A sense of adventure, curious taste buds, and good spirits are very effective rising agents, too.

* * *

Love

On Caring
for Another Being

When you start baking seriously, your life will not only become more meaningful, more tasty, and richer in carbohydrates, it will also become more loving. Nursing a sourdough is often compared to caring for a pet—but caring for a pet is so much easier. Pets are grateful and forgiving, nonjudgmental, and generous—well, dogs are. A sourdough is more like a cat: aloof, sometimes enjoying your touch but demanding of your time and attention on their terms. With a sourdough, you have a committed relationship, and the sourdough is the dominant partner. A sourdough is possessive and jealous, especially of the voluptuous, busty yeast. Sourdough is imperious. This you need to know. Adieu, freedom; so long, self-determination. No more *Maybe today, maybe tomorrow.*

From now on there will be regular meals and strict bedtime routines—not necessarily for you but for your sourdough. The top priorities in your emotional budget will be caretaking, responsibility, devotion, and diligence. Before you start something with a sourdough, you must answer some very delicate relationship questions: Are you still on a dating website? How quickly can you unsubscribe? If you can't get out right away, how will you explain to your new partner that you're still on Tinder?

Other important questions will arise: Am I cheating on my sourdough when I eat a donut? Have I crossed the line into infidelity if I imagine eating a croissant, or if I look at a photo of a bagel or read a recipe for a hot cross bun? What if I want to travel?

The Name of Love

For the sake of the stability of your relationship with your demanding new mate, it's highly recommended that you give your sourdough a name. Sharon, Bread Pitt, or Chuck are excellent choices. But if you're afraid of commitment and are unsure whether you have the strength to overcome such trepidation, you'd better think twice before you name your sourdough—because once you choose a name, love will grow. That's a given. That's psychology. That's just a fact. You will be defenseless and must surrender. Naming your sourdough significantly increases its chances of survival. You wouldn't starve someone you love, would you? (Really, what sort of a person are you?!)

Chuck's in Charge

As a mother or father of a little sourdough, you will ask yourself:

- Do I have permission to go out, even if the sourdough desires to be fed at night?
- Am I allowed to have a smoke on the balcony?
- Do I need a sourdough sitter and a sourdough baby monitor?
- Will I hear if my sourdough lets a bubble burst?
- Who will take Chuck over Christmas?
- Who will nurse him when I go on vacation?

Yes, it's possible to travel with a sourdough, but please consider, if traveling by air, that security staff and border officials may take a very dim view of a bubbly gray mass in an old jam jar. They will not be amused by your explanation that what they see is the immature form of a lovely bread. When planning vacations, you'll find yourself concerned that your sourdough might be unwell in the unfamiliar ambiance of the minibar in your tiny hotel room in a resort in Cancun.

- Will he get homesick?
- Will he find the local microbes tasty?

Imponderables are countless. Questions are enormous.

In the progressive city of Stockholm, a couple desiring rampant togetherness after living with a demanding sourdough can check their starter at a sourdough-starter hotel right by the airport. In Brooklyn, the epicenter of everything hip, you'll find a similar establishment ready to register and care for your sourdough partner. A bed-and-breakfast for your sourdough is available for as little as fifteen dollars per week. If he or she is ailing or a little frail, diagnostics, intensive care, and rehab are available on request.

But traveling to Cancun via Stockholm or Brooklyn may be a rather circuitous route for you, and one that will decimate your frequent-flyer point balance. In Germany, a nation known for its bread (which is often missed by its expats), there is the traditional, family-owned *Gasthof Sauerteig* (Sourdough Inn). Here, a room for two starts at eighty-nine euros, and the cuisine is honest, earthy, and hearty. Despite this establishment's name, only humans are welcome; there are no rooms available for sourdough starters, because they're rarely housebroken and have a tendency to make an inconvenient mess. But don't worry—once you've partnered with a sourdough, you'll find that going on vacation loses its charms anyway. In addition, the starter is a fussy traveler and a frequent complainer on the road. Remember the one place that's like no other, where you can bake all day and all night? Home Sweet Home!

Everything Is Very, Very Satisfying

So you see, there's a lot to consider before you whisk up your first sourdough starter. Please don't underestimate this! Once you've blended water and flour, there's no turning back. In the silent union of these two humble elements new life is created, inevitably, from practically nothing. From thin air, from the flour, and from those teeny-tiny microorganisms living in it. If only Dr. Frankenstein had known this! He would have become a baker. (Yes, good doctor, "It's *alive!*") He could have spared his pitiable, roughly patched-up creature so much pain and heartbreak.

Do you remember what it feels like to be a patient witness, waiting for the creation of life to occur before your very eyes? Perhaps in your childhood days, having poured a little bag of apparently dead sea monkeys into water, you felt the unrestrainable urge to jump up every other minute to check to see if the promised miracle has happened. The hope of seeing this gets you up at night, anxiously pacing, checking and rechecking your sourdough partner. Is he/she/they still breathing? Did he/she/they already grow? The meticulous attention even the most laid-back or negligent characters devote to recording a starter's growth is astounding. Appointments are canceled or forgotten for the love of your sourdough starter.

Basic needs like eating, sleeping, and constantly checking your phone for messages lose all meaning as we become attentive midwives at the delivery of a mother or father of generations of sourdough breads. Starting a starter is like falling in love. *He* is your first thought in the morning and your last before you drift off to sleep at night. You dream of *him*. It's not an exaggeration to recognize this as a consciously acquired obsessive-compulsive disorder. It is, however, a useful one, with positive side effects. What may sound like sacrifice and submission is actually a great gain. Your dopamine level rises with the prospect of a delicious reward—the joy of having made something nurturing, pure, and healthy completely by yourself, with your own clumsy hands. Can anything be more satisfying?

Be Aware of Your Mindfulness
This meticulous devotion to the object of your love may affect all areas of your daily life. While caring for a sourdough, your spirit rises, your self-exteem expands, and you nurture respect—for your fellow human beings, for this precious planet, and for your micro-collaborators on this sourdough journey. This happens without anyone having to tell you to kindly start

being a better person. In your new mindful and caregiving state, you'll find yourself doing many more easy, slow, loving, orderly things. A dedicated slob I know told me that, soon after he started baking, he began to carefully and accurately weigh not only his flour but also his words. He suddenly started paying more attention. He eschewed careless hurrying in all his actions and began to sense the comfortable temperature not only of his sourdough but of his surroundings as well. He became more empathetic, diligent, and proper. He started to undo the laces of his shoes before taking them off and began placing those shoes neatly next to each other. In the evenings he no longer tossed his clothes onto the mountain burying his poor bedside chair, waiting for the excavator at the end of each month; he began to hang his clothes on hangers and store them in the closet. He experienced a desire to improve his handwriting. He wanted to throw away the technical enzymes like smartphones, pads, and laptops that were ruling his life, or to give them to an enemy. He noticed a wish to write with a fountain pen—to write poetry and odes, or letters or postcards at the very least. He imagined writing a shopping list that sounded like poetry: rye flour, sea salt, scraper, proofing basket, thermometer. These changes in personality and behavior occurred about a month after he became hooked on the sourdough lifestyle.

Once he was infatuated, staring at Sebastian, Sybille, Samantha, or Stewart in their jam jars and sensing the tiniest stirring with the sensitivity of a seismograph eased his worried mind and opened his heart. His compassion grew to such an extent that he started to check in on his elderly neighbor, as he recognized that there were tall as well as small life-forms he could choose to nurture and support. And the hobby baker looked very well himself; he often went to bed at the same hour as the sourdough, and in the mornings he smelled fresh and healthy and looked jaunty and plump, just like his sourdough baby.

*   *   *

Sensuality

On Eyes, Ears, and Hands, and on Body Temperature, Smell, and the Abundance of Pleasant Sensations

Ask twenty-three men and nine women in a baking class; ask semiprofessional, obsessed, really good amateur bakers; or even ask the creator of this book's ultimate recipe himself: "Are you thinking about something while baking, and if so, what?"

Each will offer the same answer: "Nothing."

How disappointing! How shockingly uninspired! But is it really true? Allegedly, the baker slips into a so-called flow and, by the moment when he or she cuts the fresh bread, is unable to recall a single thought. What a rush! Bakers of all varieties, so it seems, forget everything around them, including themselves. How is that possible, when full attention is required throughout each step of the process? When one needs all five senses to be fully engaged? When there is constantly something to calculate, to measure, to weigh, and, most of all, to feel? Do they truly think of nothing? Bakers need to see, to taste, to touch, to smell, and even to hear. For an agreeable baking result, it's essential to meticulously pay attention to the temperature and keep an eye on the clock, or at least the calendar. We need to know what we're doing.

Under the Cover, Sodom and Gomorrah

The microorganisms living in a sourdough are not at all shy. They confront us with dramatic experiences, as it is beyond description what goes on in the bowl under the plastic. It's one big orgy. In fact, sourdough ought to be hidden from children's eyes. How do we explain to our kids why it's getting bigger and bigger? Should we tell them that the cute little lactic-acid bacteria living in the dough get big round bellies because they're such gluttons and because we feed them so well? Or should we tell them they're pregnant, as there is continuous copulating going on? And devouring. And digesting. And farting, too. For hours and hours. All night long. Incessantly. And it's exactly these excesses that will make the bread we bake so healthful, as—and this might be another shock to those with a sensitive disposition—these little busybodies are in the process of pre-digesting a future loaf of bread.

Tactile, sensual contact with sourdough invites the boldest

fantasies. It's gooey and sticky and makes sounds. Or it may feel celestially gentle. Imagine touching silky, weightless flour, so soft it makes us sigh and moan with bliss when we bury our hands in it, and what a pleasure to see the powdery substance fall silently into the bowl. How can one forget sensations like this? Here's my guess: these bewitching offers are a siren song to our senses, inviting them in to play; this is the reason we bake in the first place. In doing so we learn, inevitably, to become more sensitive—and sensitivity is a useful skill in dealing not only with dough but also with our loved ones. A sourdough sends out the most subtle messages. Learning to decode them is especially helpful when dealing with demanding people who expect us to read their minds. If we wish to do them this favor, at least once in a while (because we love them so much), we would be well advised to watch and listen carefully to what sourdough has to say.

Being in Ones's Senses

On the sourdough's leisurely and lengthy trip to the oven, he tells us how he feels every time we touch his sticky being. We learn to sense his emotional state by looking into his bubbles and measuring their size, and by listening to the crackling sound they make when they burst. The sound of his smacks tells us whether we've reached the point of sufficient kneading. Our nose tells us what type of personality we have before us. Does his hearty sauerkraut smell indicate he's a bit rough but an easygoing and down-to-earth kind of guy? Does he smell friendly, slightly sweet, and earthy, like grandmother's jam cellar? Or is he an edgy punk, oozing a scent reminiscent of nail polish remover? Is his smell piquant and full flavored, like hiking socks at the end of a weeklong trek? Is he a zesty, citrusy, cheerful soul, or an audacious boozehound? There are starters that smell like bratwurst or smoked bacon. Each one is different, every time.

So, never say to a sourdough, "I know you, my dear."

He will try to persuade you of that false belief. And he teaches us that it's well worth trying to look at a person we believe we know well in an open, curious, and highly attentive fashion, as if seeing him or her for the very first time—and allowing ourselves to be surprised.

You might now be getting a sense that baking sourdough bread is a truly sensuous experience. That's why we shouldn't believe bakers who claim that they don't think of anything while baking; they're just too embarrassed to talk about it. Understandable, as what we feel and think is our own private pleasure. Plus, the question was asked too carelessly. It should be put this way: "What exactly are you thinking of while tenderly and warily kneading a soft, velvety, elastic, body-warm dough? What images appear before your inner eye? And what exactly are you thinking of while tenderly and warily kneading *two* pieces of soft, velvety, elastic, body-warm dough? Nothing? Really?"

In my survey, this question generated one profoundly honest answer. One gentleman smiled dreamily, getting misty, and said, "I'm thinking of Veronica."

The Bread-Baking Man

There are countless possibilities for adults who aim to acquire or deepen personal skills and interests: workshops for self-growth, personality contouring, or becoming a better, brighter, more equanimous, friendlier, healthier, stronger, or more flexible human being. But wherever you look—French classes, the magic of watercolor, pottery, Mindfulness Based Stress Reduction (MBSR), yoga, kimchi, ikebana, Jungian analysis, quilting—you will almost always find only women! Whatever the program, the attendance will be 98 percent female.

Where are the men? What do they do? Take a wild guess: they're baking bread! That's because even a whole weekend of opening hips in a yoga workshop will not deliver a "real," tangible outcome. And this deficiency might be unsatisfactory to the goal-oriented male. In baking classes, the gender ratio is usually fifty-fifty, with a slight tendency toward a male majority. This is likely caused by the aforementioned tactile charms of baking, which resonate particularly with men, but there are further reasons that we can take into consideration. In mentioning them here, I'm fully aware of the risk of being accused of serving up annoyingly antique gender-role clichés, but here they are: the baking man radiates caring and responsibility. He's a provider and fulfills basic needs—food, warmth, sensual satisfaction. This is an image the male human likes for himself, and the female finds it attractive, too, if not sexy—and being considered sexy pleases the baking male. Baking bread has all the right curves and touches.

Sagabona Kunjani Wena

The men in baking classes are aged between twenty and eighty. They often have well-defined arms, and the more experienced ones are very adept with their hands; it's a pleasure to watch them handle things (while thinking of nothing, of course). What a joy to witness their gentle yet firm touch while handling delicate, airy, yeasty doughs for focaccia or a baguette, doughs that feel like scented, bodyless foam under the skin of a fairy. Unshapable, actually; white clouds made of water and flour. Heavenly! If this isn't suggestive, what is?

But far more challenging than handling clouds is shaping a gray rye sourdough for baking. It's very soft. Very warm. Very goopy. This dough means to very finely evaluate the strength of those well-defined arms, particularly in light of the familiar rebuke that men are predisposed toward gross motor skills only and are rarely capable of tenderness. In the matter of developing a strong yet delicate touch, here is a great opportunity to practice intensely, for the enjoyment of all stakeholders. Consider multiplying the measurements and practicing tender touches often, carefully turning the dough upside down and rounding it. Practice, practice, practice.

It's easy if you approach the dough in a very laid-back fashion, knees bent loosely, breathing full and easy, without exertion or pressure, staying relaxed. Music can be helpful; working with a rhythm. Could any song be more perfect to prepare bread than 1989's "Bakerman" by the Danish band Laid Back? Its lyrics include this unforgettable Swahili verse:

Baker man is baking bread
Sagabona kunjani wena
Baker man is baking bread
You've got to cool down, take it easy
You've got to cool down, relax, take it easy
Slow down, relax, it's too late to worry
Slow down, take it easy[1]

Mmmmmm

It's an epic moment when your bread is committed to the oven. From this point forward, scent rules the scene. Some say the smell is the main reason they bake: the delicious odor that, within minutes, fills the kitchen and the hall, flooding all the rooms and sneaking down the staircase, wafting out into the streets and hovering as a fragrant haze around the neighborhood. The smell of baking bread does something magical to anyone whose olfactory center is operational. Nobody can deny the impact of this heavenly fragrance. If only one single scent molecule arrived on the inch-square landing pad in the upper part of the nasal cavity where ten million olfactory cells yearn for stimuli, all gates would automatically open. The little bread-fragrance molecule doesn't wait in the antechamber of

1. "Bakerman," Laid Back, 1989, music/lyrics: Tim Strahl, John Guldberg.

the emotions, it simply breezes by border control and security, bypasses the neurons checking residential status and visas, and proceeds directly to the brain, where it overpowers the now smiling boss.

In the limbic system, all drawers storing memories and emotions burst open. No matter how old they are, they come alive. So alive! If a fragrance triggers something, we're disarmed. While we may suspect that the scent of freshly baked bread aims to manipulate our feelings and can even see through this ruse, we are nevertheless rendered helpless and surrender to it. Smell is the oldest of our senses, and the most underrated. It has great power over usually reasonable, intelligent *Homo sapiens*, the crown of biological creation. Maybe it's because it turns us into little animals, acting according to our instincts and letting go of having everything under control. Our nose decides who we like and with whom we want to reproduce. And when we detect the fragrance of bread, we feel nourished, protected, peaceful, safe, and secure. This is a place where people are able to relax and plan beyond the next two hours. We're home. It's the fragrance of a generous love. And if domestic peace is disturbed and we feel unable to say the words "I'm sorry" or "I love you anyway, you ox," we can, alternatively, put bread in the oven so the fragrance can speak for us. In this instance we don't need to wait for the bread to cool before cutting it. We can hug it tightly to our chest and then chop a thick slice for our beloved as if it were a piece of our own heart. We allow a pad of butter to melt on it, and all the world is good again. *Yes!*

The Best Flavor Enhancer Is Time

If there's no acute need to make up with someone and nobody is in danger of starving, do not allow your freshly baked bread to be eaten immediately. If you can curb your enthusiasm and desire for just a little longer, you will enhance the bliss. Invite the bread on a seven-day sensory-olfactory-gustatory journey— enjoy little bites over the course of a full week. You'll return with a refined sense of taste, bringing with you delightfully elegant adjectives capable of describing your experience more precisely and elaborately than the hackneyed *yummy.*

Good bread gets better every day; bad bread gets worse within hours. Fresh from the oven and wrapped in their roasting aromas, even the most miserable rolls are able to deceive us. They look so good, and our mouths cannot help but water when we carry them through the door in the evening, still warm from the automated supermarket oven; we gulp them down greedily. The next morning, we awaken to find that the bread has undergone the old Western-movie transformation: from the Good to the Bad to the Ugly. We notice a disquieting sensation in our bellies—as we so often do after purely instinct-driven encounters, when we rush to indulge and awaken with regret and remorse. The crispy-voluptuous roll that seduced us last night is now unrecognizable, dry and staler than dust on the tongue. So disillusioning! But seeing through and releasing illusions is a useful step. Now we can turn to the Good, the Beautiful, and the True. Good bread—really good bread, like the one you're going to bake—matures each and every day, developing delicate new facets to grace our senses.

A Feast for the Taste Receptors

Experienced connaisseurs are able to taste four hundred different flavors in one piece of bread, and the same bread will taste differently today, tomorrow, and in four days' time. The taste of the crust is distinct from that of the crumb. You will want to eat it with sweet creamery butter and raspberry jam for breakfast on Day One. On the evening of Day Two, it's perfect with aged gouda and a full-bodied red wine. Day Three brings enjoyment when paired with thinly sliced cucumber and red radishes, perhaps with salted butter made from sour cream and a beer on the side. And on Day Four, you finally figure it out: your bread tastes the very best when eaten without anything else, just by itself. Doing so is pure joy, and delivers the richest aromatic splendor.

To experience this blissful feeling, try the following steps. First, press freshly cut bread between your hands and inhale deeply through your nose; what emerges from the pores will amaze you. Then, dig your nose right into the soft belly of your bread. Yes, you read that correctly—come really close with that schnozzle of yours! Close your eyes . . . how does it smell? What besides *yummy* comes to mind? Rustic? Sour? Malty? Salty? Roasty? Savory? Mild? Is it fruity? Fresh fruity or dry fruity? Does it smell flowery, sweet? Are there hints of vanilla? Or is it like cabbage, caramel, or coffee? Yeasty? Meaty? Mushroomy? Earthy? Woody? Smoky? Does it smell rather moorish, as in "I want more"? Now it's time to cut a tiny piece, touch it, put it into your mouth, and chew. With this move you can be even more precise. Does it taste acidic, like balsamic vinegar? Fruity, like apple? Nutty, like chestnut, or does it remind you more of hazelnut? Your tongue and nose will be surprised by the way the taste changes with time. Precisely because bread is so mundane, it behooves us to look, smell, and taste with exquisite attention to detail.

If you set the bread's cut edge down on a wooden board, the crust will stay crisp. If you'd like to make it a little cozier, you can throw a linen cover over it, but this isn't really necessary. Handled in this fashion, it will easily last a whole week. Theoretically. If you can restrain yourself. But never, ever put it in the fridge, please. Promise!

*　　*　　*

Patience

On the Rediscovery of Lost Time and the Beauty in Waiting

Are you the type of person who jaywalks? Do you champ at the bit when your email correspondent doesn't answer before you've even hit send? Do you fuss, fidget, and freak out when waiting in line? Does it really upset you if your calming chamomile tea needs to steep for eight minutes? You can't wait for summer, and you can't wait for winter either? When the minutes until the touchdown of the plane your lover is on seem interminably gooey—like a mature wheat sourdough with excess gluten—do you go berserk? You probably couldn't curb your impatience and have already peeked at the last page of this book.

You deserve a real roasting!

If you're always trying to rush things, you definitely need another dose of Rainer Maria Rilke. Things are exactly as he writes in his letters to an impetuous young poet who feels tormented because he can't wait to be a wise old poet. Rilke pens such comforting sentences that one wants to stitch his words with manicured hands and the finest silken threads onto precious fabric to honor their wisdom, gentleness, and beauty. Rilke advises the young man to be patient, "allowing things their own silent undisturbed evolution which arises from deep inside and cannot be forced or accelerated."[1]

There you are again! And that's a practice that is so easily transferred from writing poetry to baking, and from baking to life itself.

Practice Patience

It is what it is. Things are the way they are and shall remain so as long as they need to. Dare to trust. At some point your lover's airplane will land. At some point the dough will rise. You can, with certain actions, influence the latter—with your choice of flour, with the temperature of the water you add. The room temperature can also accelerate progress, and even your mood affects the mood of your doughy housemate.

However, following a recipe with the highest degree of precision should not lead us to believe that we are truly in charge and have everything under control. Those microscopic entities in the dough will teach us to be humble and patient. We will have to adjust to the nature and wishes of the dough, not vice versa. A sourdough starter is ripe when it decides to be ripe,

1. Letter from Rainer Maria Rilke to Franz Xaver Kappus, Viareggio,
   Italy, April 23, 1903.

and that might take a while. Or it may go surprisingly quickly; sometimes it's like this, sometimes it's like that. If you keep the starter waiting, it might be too late, and then you'll have to start all over again. But, fortunately, there are worse things. Practice makes perfect. And the most crucial skill to practice is patience.

An Experience in Letting Go

Early one summer I participated in one of Master Baker Lutz Geißler's courses. It took place in his own bakery in the tiny village of Sehmatal-Cranzahl in the Ore Mountains, on the border between Germany and the Czech Republic. On close observation, one finds that the Ore Mountains in this area are not mountains but rather soft, rolling hills, with a steep cliff to one side that is called the "Mountain of Slices," or *Scheibenberg* in German. My inn was located in the village of Crottendorf, not far from the cliff and separated from Sehmatal-Cranzahl by a narrow range of hills.

Not possessing a car with which to bypass this geological peculiarity that looked like a loaf of bread cut into slices, I hiked to the bakery, five miles to the east, each morning, and hiked back five miles to the west each evening to my inn. The path crossed a stream into a dark wood where ancient spruce trees kept enormous rocks prisoner between their trunks. The wood was both enchanting and foreboding. The route continued along the Old Salt Road past golden cornfields and downhill until it crossed another stream.

"How perfect!" I said to myself. "Grain! Water! Salt! And a Bread Slice Mountain en route! All this on the way to a bakery!"

I felt wonderfully old-fashioned and bona fide, arriving each day in such a time-consuming, mindful, and environmentally friendly way at my destination, having journeyed entirely by foot. How refreshing was that?

Slowing Down Opens the Eyes

Had I traveled hastily to my baking class in an automobile, a human accelerator, I would not have noticed that the sound of beeches rustling is different from that of oaks. I would never have seen the withered signpost pointing leisurely wanderers to Murder Rock. I would have overlooked the overgrown path to the mysterious Seven Acids, and would definitely have missed the little birdhouse with the big red star standing in the wheat field, housing a Marxist-Leninist chickless chickadee couple.

Had I walked very quickly, which is my usual habit, the hike would have taken only an hour. But having read Rilke, I had learned about patience, in life and in baking. So, I put myself in the shoes of an airy focaccia dough and allowed myself to take a little longer. Experimenting with my walking speed led to an important insight: taking it slow is good! Not only for dough but also for humans. We need to find our own, individual speed in life. The pace we walk is the pace we should choose for most everything else we do. If we hurry and rush, we will make ourselves anxious—ourselves and those around us. It's as if we put ourselves in alarm mode.

However, if we reduce our speed even minimally from an average of five feet per second to four feet per second, we welcome ease and maximize well-being. If your natural speed is already a snail's pace, please beware! Here, too, there are similarities between doughs and humans. Each needs some body tension and a willingness to grow. Without that, we will not get anywhere.

*　*　*

Focus

On the Enthralling Pleasure
of **Radical Monotasking**

The desire to juggle numerous tasks is understandable, because busy *Homo sapiens* like efficiency very, very much. But what is multitasking good for in the end?

Nothing. Nada. Diddly-squat.

What good is the reversible jacket?

The pant-skirt?

The sofa bed?

The first two look indecisive and rarely fit well. The remaining culprit is comfortable neither for sitting nor for sleeping, and aesthetically the sofa bed leaves us utterly dissatisfied. However, the most dubious invention to boost efficiency and time saving is the to-go coffee cup. Only if it's a question of life or death is there the need to do two things at once or to hurry: if it's ovulation day or if the sourdough is in danger of starving.

Slow Down! Quickly!
Why is it that the whole world is talking about slowing down,

while at the same time people are consuming their lovely hot beverages on the double? If you add your average walking speed of, say, 3 miles an hour to 1,000 miles an hour—the rotation speed of our planet[1]—it adds up to having a coffee at approximately 1/6,000,000 the speed of light.

There will be spillage. There will be stains! Having a coffee while walking is diametrically opposed to the very idea of having a coffee. Having a coffee means stopping, sitting down, pausing. And most of all, it means having a coffee.

These days, modern humans not only drink coffee while walking; they consume whole menus. With sauces and sides. While checking one or two or five accounts on a dumb smartphone and actively not listening to a podcast on mindfulness from the deceleration app on their other dumb device. Because in their minds, they're already in the next meeting or in the meeting following that one, or back in the one before—anywhere but here and now.

Be Where You Are

We who are not present in the time and place we actually inhabit miss life. If we aren't present in these precious, unique, unrepeatable, irreversibly gone moments of our being—a

---

1. This is Einstein's Theory of Relativity, by the way.

wonder in itself—we miss the complete opulence of the present moment. If we're somewhere else, hastily consuming coffee on the go, here are some of the things we may miss:

- The sky is sky blue.
- A fellow human being smiles.
- The first cherries are here.
- There are so very many shades of green.
- The magpies have babies.
- The distant traffic sounds like the Atlantic off Biarritz.
- A tiny hair is tickling my ear.
- My sock is slipping.
- I want to sing.
- A beautiful lady is wearing a beautiful dress and lily-of-the-valley perfume.
- Behind an open window someone is playing Chopin's Nocturne in C-sharp Minor, op. 20.
- Fine sand is scrunching under the leather soles of expensive shoes.
- The coffee is a blend of 73 percent Indonesian and 27 percent Vietnamese beans that have been roasted for 19.2 minutes in a copper vat at 270°F and brewed with 189°F double-filtered water.

Delicious, delicious, delicious.

But unnoticed.

Do What You Do

What does this chapter, which does not mention even a single slice of bread (not a crumb!), want to tell you? That nothing good comes out of being in a hurry and doing more than one thing at a time. No good bread in particular.

If your head is in a different time zone than your feet in the present moment, you'll need a lot of luck baking bread. But if you're the kind of person who's scatterbrained, panting and speeding through life, sourdough is exactly the guru to teach you beatific monotasking.

This time-consuming activity, which requires interest, love, watching, listening, and full engagement of all the senses, will do you good.

Baking offers countless opportunities to practice awareness of the present tense. It puts you in a peaceful mood and qualifies as a life meditation. One of the most joyous and calming exercises is delivering the bread to the oven and then sitting with your spine in an upright position in front of the oven window. You can do this cross-legged, in a lotus position, or in a chair.

The key ingredient is that you're comfortable, so that your mind doesn't rush to the end of the sitting. Now let your gaze, through half-closed eyelids, rest on your soft, pale-gray dough baby and observe its transformation into a glorious, vigorous, deep-brown, confident rye bread.

Inhale. Exhale.

Inhale. Exhale.

Straighten your back again.

Lift the sternum and feel a little proud.

The duration of this oven-action-movie meditation should be no less than forty-five minutes.

*　　*　　*

Generosity

On the Sharing of Joy

It is the same with all important things: we cannot possess them. That's why we cannot own beauty. We cannot keep the truth to ourselves. Love, the sun, the moon, and the stars—they belong to everybody. It's the same with air, the sound of waves crashing on the seashore, and the scent of flowers. The wind that tousles a field of rye and makes it look like rippling fur—this miracle is never yours. It isn't mine or anybody else's. We can't claim ownership of a good heart. Neither does a really good joke or really good bread truly belong to us.

These things are meant to be shared. What a joy it is to give someone bread you've baked, and what bliss it is to receive. There are bakers whose main purpose and greatest source of happiness is making family and friends, neighbors, and other hungry folks happy with their baking. For the rye bread recipe in this book, the price of the ingredients and the energy needed equals approximately one dollar. What a wondrous and flavorful example of the so often forgotten distinction between the worth of an item and its value. Not only in the economic realm but also in the emotional one, giving bread produces an extremely advantageous relationship between expenditure and income. The glow in the eyes of the recipient of home-baked bread is priceless.

A Sourdough Starter Belongs to Everyone

If you dare to give the gift of life to a sourdough, you must also learn to let go of your little one. Yes, even though it was exhausting to parent him; yes, despite the sleepless nights and the constant fear that he or she (though it seems to me that sourdough starters are mostly boys and leavened doughs are girls) might collapse and turn into a soggy flatbread (teen-agers!). The day will come when your sourdough starter wants to reproduce and multiply—that is his nature. And it will not take long for that day to arrive! He will want to do it with every-one. He will want to make babies with each and every lactic-acid bacteria and yeast spore that's roaming around, and he will want his babies to make more babies.

If your sourdough starter is grown enough to stand on his own two feet, let him go. Give him away. Trade and bestow him in small portions that are sufficient to bake two pounds of hap-piness. Find the like-minded and the needy and provide them with your hot microbiological stuff. You'll recognize anonymous sourdough activists in the crowd. In exchange, you might receive Russian or Austrian or Israeli sourdough starters that will create the most interesting encounters with the guy you have at home. Chuck will be thrilled to meet Boris, Helmut, or Shlomo! There will be nights when you'll have to rescue desperate soon-to-be-hooked-on-sourdough souls; when they whisper the code "*Lactobacillus plantarum, Lactobacillus brevis, et Saccharomyces cerevisiae . . .*" you will generously slide them a dose of your starter. They will be over the moon to be able to start baking the same night! Because once the decision to begin baking is made, the days waiting for a starter to be ripe feel endless and too painful to bear.

Welcome a Stranger into Your House

None of the loaves baked from the sourdough starter you gave away or received from others will look and taste like your first one. Each new sourdough will be different from his father, because he adapts himself to the new domain, the new atmosphere, the new people, and the new flora and fauna in the air around him. No bread you bake will be like any other.

*   *   *

Authenticity

On a Positive Attitude toward Negative Film, **Whole-Grain Photopaper, and Good Luck**

To bake a completely natural, earthy, artisan bread, you need four ingredients: flour, water, salt, and time. And what is needed to take an authentic photo of such a loaf? A digital dual-lens reflex camera? A nefarious food stylist trained in alchemy and deception? A minimum of 9,749 shots from which to pick 19? Perhaps, to finish it off, adding excessive amounts of Photoshop and a large serving of hipster retro filters?

Seriously?

Such an approach is as tasteless and dishonest as bread from a gas station. Taking photos of our bread in this way would be the equivalent of using technical enzymes, baking powder, and artificial flavors in an automatic baking machine. This is the opposite of everything this book holds precious: the quiet contentedness of patience, honesty, and chance.

Digital photography? Traitorous! We choose integrity! We choose to be consistent and authentic in each step of the process! That's why the photographic images in this book were produced with the same attitude and at a similar speed as the breads they display, savoring long phases for development and risking imperfection for the sake of purity and truth.

What a Beautiful Development

Each bread has its own identity, absolutely unique—and so does each photograph in this book. The images, just like the breads, are not a data set but real, analog depictions that are fully authentic, in the flesh—or, rather, the paper. They were shot with real light hitting real photographic film. This forgotten material consists of a transparent polyester base coated on one side with a light-sensitive emulsion containing microscopic silver halide crystals. These rolls of film were hard to come by. Some of them had been sitting in the photographer's fridge for decades—just like some forgotten sourdough starter—somewhere in the unexplored regions behind the apricot jam and the anchovies with best-by dates approaching the last millennium.

These rolls were tired—very tired—but they were alive. They were developed in a darkroom by a living, breathing human being. Copies were fabricated by hand. Each image is the result of meticulous conceptual, artisanal, artistic groundwork, not mischievous computer manipulation. Some of the photos were even produced with one of the simplest ingredients in the history of photography: the pinhole camera. As good bread consists of only water, flour, and salt, these images were made from light, light-sensitive material, and a black box.

Everything else in these photographs is honest and real, too: Lutz Geißler himself and eight passionate amateur bakers baked all the beauties in this book. While wonderfully diverse, all the loaves were baked according to the one single recipe laid out in words and images in the pages you now hold. Some of these loaves are sons and daughters, grandnephews and grandnieces of Lutz's (still unnamed!) sourdough starter—a sourdough starter who celebrated his eleventh birthday in the summer of the year this book was first published. And as there was zero food styling nor other such deceptive tomfoolery employed in our food shoot, you may rest assured that all of the bread has been joyfully consumed—with friends, with family, with or without butter. And, to be honest, not particularly slowly.

*   *   *

Lust

Recipe
and Instructions

Whether the day is sunny or gray and whether your mood is sunny or gray, gray is the color of the 100 percent rye dough that will become your two pounds of happiness. You will be amazed by the rich, full, deep, malty-brown tan that your gray dough will display when you take it out of the oven. It might be the first bread you bake. It hopefully will not be the last. Perhaps this will mark the beginning of a passionate, loving, lifelong relationship.

You'll Be Able to Bake with
One Hand Tied behind Your Back

Despite our fears and trepidation, baking bread actually requires only a small serving of time and a tablespoon of planning. If, for example, you make it your Friday-evening habit to mix the ingredients listed in the recipe below, you'll have the whole night off. The whole night! On Saturday morning, around seven or eight o'clock, you'll invest two more minutes to mix the final dough. If you're mixing by hand, you need to calculate two more minutes to free your mixing hand from the dough with the clean one. This adds up to seven minutes of work. And now, both you and the dough can rest. Or, for half an hour, you can do something else, something nice, something useful.

After this thirty-minute break, you will shape the dough for another two minutes. Then let your dough do whatever he wants. As a rule, he will want to rise. Meanwhile, you can write poetry, clean the house, meditate, practice Pilates, educate your children, manage your stock portfolio, or watch the clouds drift by. Or you can observe the oven preheating. The next step requires ten seconds, to deposit your creation in the oven, and ten more to take it out again, about an hour later. This adds up to a total active time commitment of nine minutes and twenty seconds. Surely you can spare this amount of time to produce two pounds of happiness.

The Recipe
for Your Sourdough Starter

From a humble mixture of water and flour, the mighty creator of bread dynasties of all colors and sizes and shapes will spring forth. If you don't have the time or the patience to cultivate your own starter, please consult chapter 7, "Generosity," beginning on page 53. There are always folks who have too much of everything . . .

All you need is:

50 grams (⅓ cup) whole rye flour
60 grams (60 milliliters or ¼ cup) water (122°F)

Put the water and flour in a jar with a lid or into a bowl. Stir with a spoon until you create the consistency of soft mortar. Cover, and let your sourdough starter rest—preferably in a warm (82°F to 89°F) place, but protect him from drying out. You may place him close to a gentle heat source (such as on top of the ventilation slots of the fridge). He will also feel very cozy basking in the warmth of the light bulb in the oven or microwave (do not turn the oven or microwave on!). In the summer he would love to rock with you in the garden swing under the shady trees. In any season he could also join you in the sauna or, without hesitation, the lusty fellow would come to bed with you.

Each time the mix has doubled in size, add another fifty grams of rye flour and sixty grams of warm water and mix thoroughly. It's hard to predict how long it may take for this process to get underway. It depends on the nature of the flour and the temperatures involved. It can happen within a day, or it may take several days. The sourdough should always be fed before he becomes depressed and caves in.

Freshly ground flour invites the starter to ripen more quickly. In the first twelve hours of this journey, he may be vigorously stirred with a spoon to add oxygen to the drama. The prolific yeasts and lactic-acid bacteria exhibit a particularly enthusiastic response to such stimulation.

If feeding is becoming too stressful because the starter stops rising, complains of hunger, and needs to be fed more frequently, he can be thwarted. Take only a small portion (five to fifty grams) of sourdough starter and combine it in a new jar with fifty grams of flour and sixty grams of water. The less you use, the longer you can rest until he doubles in size.

After three to five days of warmth and feeding, the sourdough starter should smell pleasantly sour and fruity. Now it's time for his last supper. By this stage he will have grown by about half of his original size and will fill a small screw-top jar. And now, off to the fridge!

In the first weeks of his life, the starter may not show his full capacity. He may need to grow up, to learn, and to shape his character. The more often he is used, the stronger and more stable the outcome.

The minute you send the starter to the fridge he will officially be called Mature Sourdough Culture. As this designation suggests, this grown-up starter is able to start a new sourdough. The recipe on page 64, for example, needs sixty grams of mature sourdough starter to produce the amount of sourdough required for a rye loaf within twelve hours.

After twelve hours, remove fifty grams from your final dough as a starter for your next loaf—taking away the same amount you added twelve hours before. Put it in the fridge. You can use this within the next week to start a new sourdough. If you can't manage to bake once a week, it's easy to keep your Mature Sourdough Culture alive (see page 69).

Leftover sourdough is a feast for the inhabitants of a compost heap. You can also add any extraneous portions to the irrigation water for everything that grows in your garden. One hundred grams of sourdough per ten liters (about two and a half gallons) of water results in a nourishing garden tonic. Sourdough is also a wonderful flavor enhancer in yeast pastry, short crusts, pasta and pizza doughs, crepes, and cooked desserts of all kinds. Five to ten grams of sourdough per one hundred grams of flour can do amazing things.

The Sourdough

300 grams (2.07 cups) wholemeal rye flour
360 grams (360 milliliters or 1.27 cups) water at 122°F
6 grams salt (a generous teaspoon — 1.054 teaspoons,
to be exact)
60 grams (½ cup) starter, your new creation or old, do-
nated, scrounged, traded, bought, or stolen

Mix the ingredients together with a spoon to a smooth consistency and then let it ripen for twelve hours at Northwest European room temperature (about 68°F; no air-conditioning!). The dough should roughly double in size in this time and smell agreeably sour; the surface should not collapse. If that happens, it's not a catastrophe — the bread will just turn out a bit more sour. If your sourdough does not expand at all, take it as a welcome exercise in patience (see page 53) and give him the time he needs to blossom.

The Final Dough

All of the above sourdough
150 grams (⅝ cup) water at 212°F
6 grams salt (a generous teaspoon — 1.054 teaspoons,
to be exact)
300 grams (2.07 cups) wholemeal rye flour

Note: Before You Start!
Take from the new sourdough the amount you added to it before
(sixty grams/half a cup), put it in a jar with a lid, and store it in the
coldest spot in your fridge until the next baking day; this is the
starter for your next sourdough adventure.

1. Pour the boiling water into a bowl and add the salt. Sprinkle
the flour on top of the water to shield the dough from too much
heat. Carefully place the remaining sourdough on the flour.

2. Mix all of the ingredients in the bowl using a robust spoon or
spatula, or mix with a machine. As a beginner, you should use
your hand in order to get a feel for the whole process. Please
note, hand is singular! You'll be doing yourself a huge favor by
not using both hands, because the dough is very (very!) sticky,
and with two sticky hands, you'll be stuck. The mixing will take

two to five minutes, or longer if you're enjoying it! The dough will be neither offended nor pleased, as he's rather dispassionate about being handled longer.

3. *The consistency* of the mix should resemble sticky mortar and be a little warmer than body temperature. If the dough is too compact, by all means add some lukewarm water. Depending on the quality of the rye flour, the dough might be able to bind with less water, so it's wise to add a little less water to begin with (twenty-five grams/twenty-five milliliters, for example) before adding more if the dough still feels too firm.

4. *Let the dough* rest for about thirty minutes at room temperature. During this period of time it should barely rise at all.

5. *Please be very* gentle shaping the dough. Get yourself and the dough into the mood to grow and mature. Music may help serve this purpose. For example, playing "Bakerman," the song with the Swahili line mentioned in chapter 4 (see page 30) — "Baker man is baking bread / *Sagabona kunjani wena*" — might help you gently shape the dough with its soothing rhythm. Very important: Sprinkle a thick layer of flour onto your work surface, and dust your hands as well. Place the dough as compactly as possible in front of you. With your dominant floured hand, very

gingerly lift the dough on the side farthest from you upward and toward the middle, pressing very lightly, while placing your other hand at the edge closest to you to stabilize it without imposing pressure. Doughs are like human beings: too much pressure blocks the desired unfolding.

6. Now turn the dough clockwise a little — or counterclockwise, if you prefer, but stick to one direction — and repeat this procedure. Sing or hum to guide the process, and never cease breathing! Repeat this movement until the dough is sleek on the underside and looks roundish, like a ball. Again: do not press too vigorously, otherwise you risk creating a great big mess and gooey flatbread.

7. Place the more or less globular dough piece on parchment paper. Now you may decide on the general crust design of your bread. If you bake it with the sleek underside turned up, the crust will display an elegant, fine veining. If the sleek side remains facedown, the crust will appear rustic, rough, and wild. Sprinkle flour on whichever side you choose to be the upper one and carefully smooth it out. Cover the dough with a bowl or a pot and leave it alone for a minimum of forty-five to sixty minutes at room temperature (68°F). He needs some space under the covering because he's planning to increase his size by half. His surface will be furrowed by ⅛- to ½-inch-wide cracks. If your dough doesn't look like this after his rest, allow him a little more time to get ready, and allow yourself to trust your feelings . . .

8. Meanwhile, no less than thirty minutes before you embark upon baking, preheat a baking sheet in the oven to 480°F–520°F. Place the sheet on a shelf in the lower third of the oven.

9. With the help of a thin wooden board or some other thin, heat-resistant item, slide the dough with the parchment paper onto the hot baking sheet. The parchment paper should stay with the dough, but by all means, pull out the wooden board! Immediately reduce the temperature to 450°F and bake the bread for sixty to sixty-five minutes to a rich dark brown. Now switch off the oven and open the oven door slightly in order to let the bread bake for another ten minutes in the decreasing heat, developing its lovely strong crust!

10. Transfer the bread to a rack to cool, allowing air to flow all around the loaf while you enjoy the heavenly aroma. Provided you have superhuman self-discipline, you will not cut the bread earlier than tomorrow, because good bread gets better every day, and one more day of maturing will tease out flavor facets; also, the sourdough tartness will relax and become milder.

Making More Sourdough

It may occur that you require more sourdough starter than what remains in your fridge. In this case, the starter needs to be multiplied like the sweet porridge in the fairy tale of the same name by the Brothers Grimm. However, no spell is needed—it's so much easier. Simply feed the sourdough more of its favorite food. What happens next is magic.

To create one hundred grams (a scant half cup) of starter:
5 grams old sourdough or starter
45 grams wholemeal rye flour
45 to 50 grams/milliliters water at 122°F

Mix all of the ingredients together and let them mature at about 86°F until the starter has approximately doubled in volume. This takes six to ten hours. In this fashion, sourdough can be multiplied infinitely. If, for example, you need 1 kilogram (2.2 pounds) of sourdough or Mature Sourdough Culture, simply use 45 to 50 grams (about ¼ cup) of old sourdough per 400 to 450 grams /milliliters each of water and flour (3¼ to 3⅝ cups).

If you cannot bake your rye bread on a weekly basis, your starter still needs to be fed! If you work with fifty grams of starter, simply halve the ingredients listed above.

Take a little courage, *an old screw-top jar, water, flour, and faith in the ways of the world — mix well.*

This is what it looks like *when a sourdough starter is aiming for higher goals: being the founder of a dynasty of zesty sourdoughs, for example.*

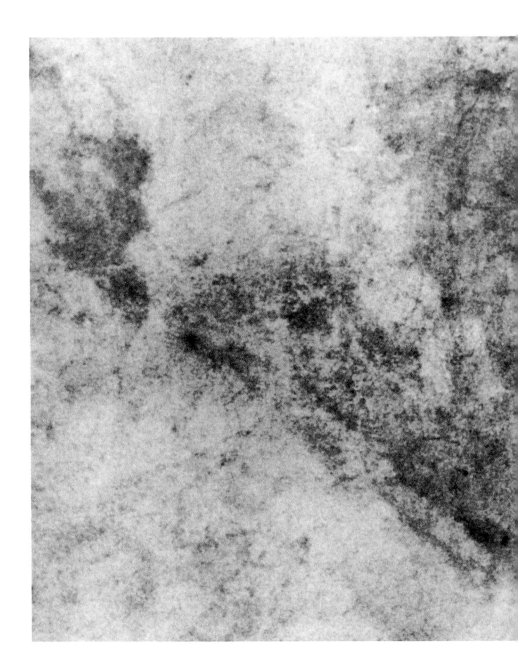

This lazy lump of rye sourdough is a wise guru. *He teaches us to patiently sit and allow something to arise. He knows his time will come.*

Practicing gentleness *promotes more than the well-being of your dough. It also benefits all other living beings with whom you are in contact. And perhaps also those with whom you would like to be in contact . . .*

One last nap *for the dough before the launch into its great transformational trip in the oven. You'll see—it's really not that difficult to initiate a fundamental change.*

Rye bread No 1. **Name of the sourdough:** *No name* **Hometown:** *Seevetal, Germany*
Family history: *Son of Lutz Geißler's sourdough (*2009)* **Cohabitants since** *July
2014* **Diet:** *rye flour type 1150 or freshly ground rye, fed every 10 days* **Baker:** *Iris
Emmrich*

Rye bread No 2. **Name of the sourdough:** *Irma Jager Memorial Dough* **Hometown:** *Hamburg, Germany* **Family history:** *Mighty successor of countless homegrown, later starved or moldy sourdoughs between 2007 and 2015* **Cohabitants since** *2016, after a restart* **Diet:** *Demeter wholemeal rye, finely ground* **Baker:** *Frank Rosin*

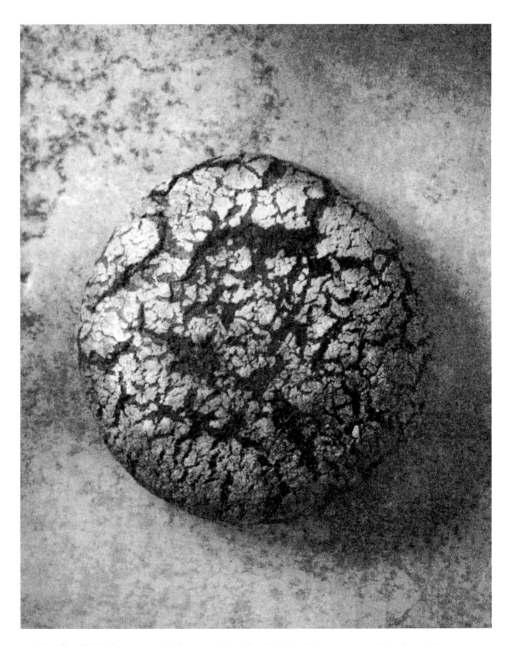

Rye bread No 5. **Name of the sourdough:** *The Rye* **Hometown:** *Hamburg, Germany* **Family history:** *Self-bred from organic wholemeal rye flour* **Descendants:** *5 children in Thuringia, North Frisia, Berlin, Düsseldorf, and Henstedt-Ulzburg, all in Germany* **Cohabitants since** *2015* **Diet:** *water and rye flour every 2 to 20 days* **Baker:** *Doreen Brodersen*

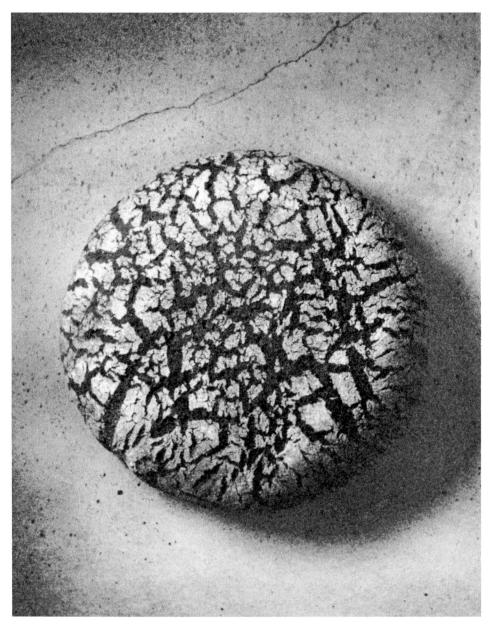

Rye bread No 4. **Name of the sourdough:** *Richard* **Hometown:** *Hamburg, Germany* **Family history:** *Home-bred following instructions in a sourdough internet forum* **Descendants:** *4 children were adopted out* **Cohabitants since** *January 2011* **Diet:** *rye flour type 1150 once a week on different days* **Baker:** *Kerstin Hansen*

Rye bread No 5. **Name of the sourdough:** *Depends; sometimes Bernd* **Hometown:** *Cologne, Germany* **Family history:** *Home birth in a picnic bag warmed with a hot water bottle* **Descendants:** *7 children in the Rhine area, in Hanover, and Barcelona, Spain* **Cohabitants since** *January 2017* **Diet:** *rye flour, Monday to Friday, late evenings* **Baker:** *Friederike Jakobs*

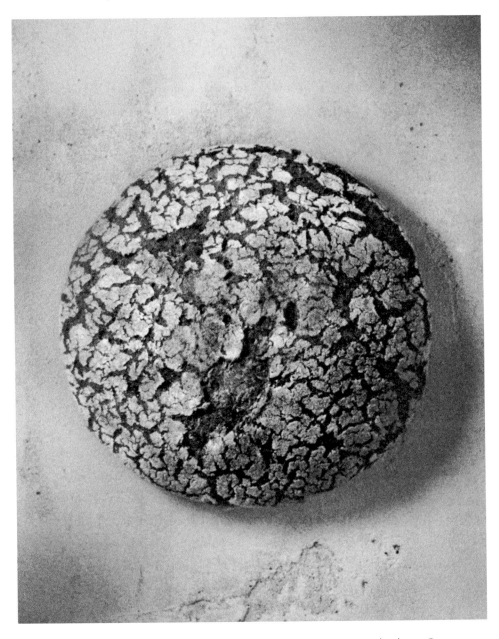

Rye bread No 6. **Name of the sourdough:** *Baby* **Hometown:** *Elmshorn, Germany*
Family history: *Self-bred* **Descendants:** *1 child at the workplace* **Cohabitants since**
Winter 2015 **Diet:** *organic rye flour type 1370 at 82°F in the light of the (switched off!)*
microwave, occasional injections with turbo-starter from a baking course or a few drops of
organic apple juice Monday to Friday, late evenings **Baker:** *Thomas Muschke*

Rye bread No 7. **Name of the sourdough:** *Monsieur* **Hometown:** *Henstedt-Ulzburg, Germany* **Family history:** *Descendant of an 18-year-old culture from the hands of a pro* **Descendants:** *Madame, a wheat sourdough* **Cohabitants since** *February 22, 2013* **Diet:** *wholemeal rye flour or type 1150 approximately 3 times within 2 weeks* **Baker:** *Ilona Schlömann*

It's a feast *to discover the taste of your own bread with eyes closed and no toppings.*

Do Not! *Do not eat the bread fresh from the oven! Wait at least a day. If the required superhuman self-discipline is not within your power, and you have a good knife, good salt, and cold butter, you will be forgiven.*

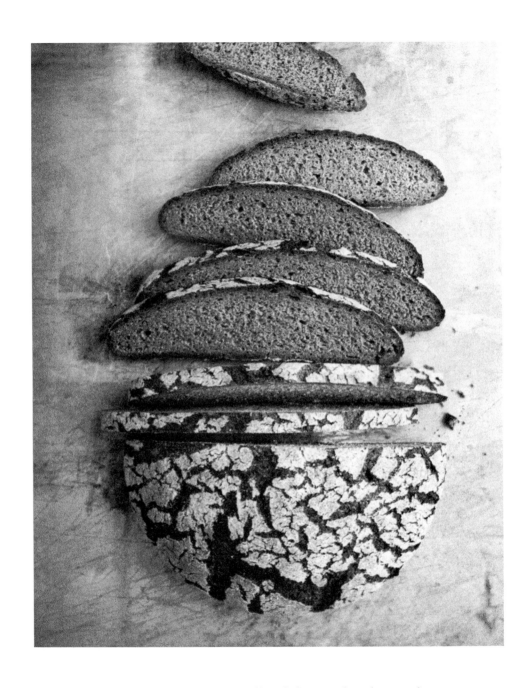

Two pounds of happiness *will easily last a week. At least, in theory.*

Accept the invitation *to come a little closer and explore the aromatic depths of the crust.*

Calming the Mind

What a day that was eighty-seven emails well thank you anything else I can do for you just do this and just do that not a minute even for a coffee if it goes on like this I wonder how it goes with the old professor I must call him I didn't accomplish what was on my list nothing gets finished and whoosh it's the evening and why does it take so long for the car to be fixed riding the bike is healthier anyway but my they're speeding like lunatics it's frightening as if they were going to war those with a helmet and saddlebags they are the worst they're homicidal so righteous relax I should relax says the doctor ride the bike haha throw the wheel what about swimming yoga meditation some kind of craft something using your hands dancing you should dance or just don't do anything for a change great idea and when I ask that's a laugh my day only has twenty-four hours I haven't been to the theater in ages but why do they always get naked onstage that's annoying or the opera ages great advice really that's a joke my boss he's a joke he can't even tell a joke he ruins every punch line how painful that was the other day but he made it to the boardroom I really don't get it I used to get along with my cousin way better than nowadays well people change why does she like that awful movie it's really no good at all she's eating totally gluten-free now hmm I don't know it seems a little excessive she should google FODMAP I couldn't live without bread a really good rye bread with a thick layer of cold salted butter and honey that's heaven it's the absolute best in the basement there's a complete set of photo equipment and the easel and the train set and the ten-thousand-piece jigsaw puzzle of the Grand Canyon my goodness the books so many books I need to live to 120 to be able to read all those books really high time to relax my doctor is right or what about doing something purposeful who wants to throw away books I really should declutter I should should should should I should have a hobby something that instantly makes me happy all the things I should I don't want to should anything at all that'd be wonderful to let myself go just lie there fat and lazy and good for nothing and rest and the sun would warm my belly and there's nothing for me to do and I'll get all light and soft like a cloud I was a kid when I did that the last time lying on the lawn behind the music school watching the cloud castles and mountains and valleys of cotton candy and feather giants horsemen elephants beautiful women what's her name again she's practicing mindfulness now they practice eating a raisin in that course like with emotion and sensitivity and all and their eyes closed I tried it out there's something to that you see a raisin with new eyes when you keep them closed while eating and they are also practicing to be in the here and now well where else can you be although it's true often the mind is miles away you lose your place where on earth did I put the scales again I better wear an apron hopefully there's some flour in the house it's great I don't need anything else but flour they're also practicing breathing seriously I can do that I can breathe even with my eyes closed and in my sleep in out in out in out that's easy it's automatic who needs a course for that anyway I'll weigh the flour now and heat up the water and then I'll get Bread Pitt out of the fridge he's all excited too already and then I'll watch him making bubbles I wonder what those bubbles actually are there's nothing I'd rather do than watch Bread Pitt get fatter and fatter and not think about anything while watching him but what a friendly warm gray that is and plop another bubble I beg your pardon Bread Pitt did you break wind and I imagine how happy everybody will be when I'm baking tomorrow morning mmmmmm how good that smells I'll bake five loaves that's a piece of cake oh man such a homemade sourdough bread that's the best thing in the world and you can learn a lot from Bread Pitt he doesn't think that much and the outcome is always good he just takes his time that's the be-all and end-all and all is good.

Gratitude

There Are So Many
Wonderful People!

If baking bread is not accessible to you at a certain point in your life journey—because you're too busy making dough, for example, or too busy loafing or pursuing other pie-in-the-sky ideas—there are alternative approaches to achieving happiness. These are available to anybody, anytime, anywhere, practically each and every minute we walk the planet consciously; even amid the activities mentioned above.

Practicing gratitude is a very effective method, and it requires no equipment at all—just some mental energy and kind thoughts. It's recommended to practice gratitude as if it were a lower-back exercise or a biceps workout. For, in truth, the heart is a muscle, too, so it can be trained!

Try to feel gratitude for waking up in the morning.

For being able to think all these luxurious, idle thoughts.

For holding this little book in your hands—a book that is the work of many!

My heart expands like a happy sourdough thinking of the seven enthusiastic co-humans who selflessly supported the idea of this book. Recruited at short notice via Lutz Geißler's baking blog, they baked two pounds of happiness following the book's single recipe. They created the seven beautiful, diverse, and unique bread personalities that you find portrayed in these pages.

A big thank-you to Doreen Brodersen, Iris Emmrich, Kerstin Hauser, Friederike Jakobs, Thomas Muschke, Frank Rosin, and Ilona Schlömann.

And a very special, oven-warm thank-you to Christina Weiß, who made us very happy with all the other beautiful loaves that posed in front of our analog cameras—in the nude!

I'm grateful that my German publisher gave me—once again—the greatest freedom and chose to embark on this adventure, whose outcome was uncertain. Thank you, Ralf Joest.

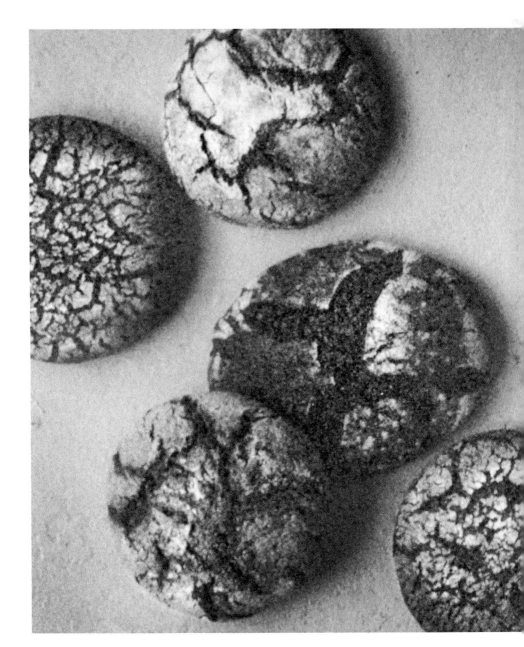

One single recipe. *Seven unique breads. Fourteen pounds of happiness.*

Team Spirit

How to Bake a Book:
Write, Knead, Shoot

Judith Stoletzky

The author acknowledges that writing describes her occupation correctly but insufficiently, because she not only produces words to fill the pages in a book but also creates a recipe for the look and feel of it.

She confesses that during the making of this book, sourdoughs were harmed. She mistreated, neglected, and starved several in her empirical studies, overfed others, and is now nurturing her guilty conscience with crispy wholemeal pangs of remorse.

She is currently cohabiting with a descendent of Lutz Geißler's sourdough named Bruno (pronounced the French way), but she can't resist indulging in occasional escapades with leavened doughs.

Life Lessons from a Homemade Sourdough Starter is her fourth book. The other ones also deal with the pursuit of happiness, using other recipes: by practicing yoga, by cooking, or by making a mess.

Lutz Geißler

Chapter 4, "Sensuality," explains why it is wise to disbelieve everything baking men say. It came as a shock to realize that this rule also applies to Lutz himself. He claims he can't write, despite the fact that he writes one book after another. Big, thick ones, too. He has published eleven books about bread baking—so far. In addition to this, he consults with and teaches both amateurs and pros, the bread industry and gourmet chefs. You'll find him in his bakery in the Ore Mountains today and perhaps in Asia tomorrow. Most amazingly, he always finds time to bake, because he tremendously enjoys his own bread. He must know a secret to extend his days beyond twenty-four hours, somehow. His blog, www.ploetzblog.de, answers every question anyone might ever have about baking bread. His blog's single imperfection—being written in German—will soon be eliminated, as an English translation will be available!

Hubertus Schüler

This notable still-life and food photographer knows all the tricks of the trade, plus two or three more. Asking him to put his digital superpowers aside—to not use his super high-tech equipment to make our sourdough loaves look perfect—may sound quirky. And it is!

When asked to go back over one thousand years in the evolution of photography and use a pinhole camera, and then to go back over a hundred years to use an analog camera and film—for nonnegotiable aesthetic and conceptual reasons—Hubertus was instantly delighted. And then he wasn't. He cursed the fathers of photography, from Ibn al-Haytham and Leonardo da Vinci to Louis Daguerre. He swore to give up photography and turn to painting. And then he was happy again, having embarked on this artistic adventure.